GRACE DOWN BELOW

When Illness Strikes

John E. Mott Jr.

authorHOUSE®

AuthorHouse™
1663 Liberty Drive
Bloomington, IN 47403
www.authorhouse.com
Phone: 833-262-8899

Published by AuthorHouse   09/02/2021

ISBN: 978-1-5049-3315-5 (sc)
ISBN: 978-1-5049-3316-2 (e)

Print information available on the last page.

This book is printed on acid-free paper.

Illustrated by Sister Maria Vigil

Dedication

I dedicate this book to my dear brother, the late Thomas Eugene Mott. Your short lived life inspires me each and every day. And because you were determined to overcome a major illness, so was I. I love you my dear brother.

Introduction

Life has its uncertainties and there's no way around it. Wherever you go or whatever you do, there's always the element of surprise. From premature births to freak accidents, these things do occur. And as a child, I was told to always expect the unexpected.

On March 28th, 2009, my life changed dramatically and I was clueless. Once I became aware of it, I was dumbfounded! My life had taken a turn for the worst and I had no idea. At the age of 25, I was a healthy young man, but yet, I had a brain hemorrhage which caused a stroke. There were no warning signs.

I've always been up for a challenge, but this encounter topped them all. The element of surprise struck me without a trace. I was left helpless. I was at the mercy of its relentless blows. I was in for the fight of my life.

What occurred as an uncertainty was also my life's defining moment. It was nothing shy of a miracle.

I've faced many obstacles from the initial impact of the stroke to the transitional stages of my recovery.

Despite the setbacks, I made rapid improvements, but not without a struggle. My life has never been the same since my encounter. From past to present, I have had my moments. And as you read this book, my hopes are for you to be inspired.

Chapter One

A Move In Progress

It was bright and early this particular Saturday. The alarm clock sounded, so I rolled over to hit the snooze button. Within minutes I made up my bed, said a quiet prayer and gathered my things. Afterwards, I made my way to the bathroom to freshen up. For the sake of time I skipped out on breakfast. I was expecting Ally to pull up at any moment so I waited anxiously.

Ally was one of my fellow church members. She asked me to assist her in the process of moving. Moments later, Ally pulled up and blew the horn so I made my way outside.

"Good morning Deacon Mott." She said. She smiled at me as I entered into the vehicle.

"Hey! Good morning." I replied. I closed the car door as I buckled my seat belt. She put the car in drive and we made our way to her old residence.

After we pulled up to her old residence, we greeted the others and entered the apartment. I smiled with a sigh of relief when I saw that other men were present. I did a quick scan and as we conversed, we had begun the moving process. It was a total of eight people involved; there were three adult males, two younger males and three adult women.

My eyes grew big at how much stuff she had. There were three rooms jam packed with furniture, from wall to wall. We had the two younger males gather the smaller furniture while the adult males handled the bigger items. All the while, the ladies grabbed the bags and smaller boxes, which made the process so much easier.

Our main focus was to get the heavy furniture on the U-Haul truck first. We broke down the beds, dressers, and other large furniture and took them to the truck. Within minutes we cleared out the two smaller rooms and then we tackled the master bedroom. While the men handled the furniture, the women cleaned up afterwards.

After a while, the U-Haul truck was full so we shut the door and prepared to take the first load. Right before we left a concern came about, whether to eat then or later. We came to a unanimous decision...to work first and eat later. We were determined to get it over with. And off we went to the new residence.

I thought the hard part was over but I was sadly mistaken. When we arrived at the new residence we backed up the U-Haul and let down the ramp. To my surprise, there were stairs, plenty of stairs. We began to unload the U-Haul truck immediately. The apartment was spacious and beautiful. On another note, I became a skeptic; there is no way all of this furniture will fit. I thought to myself.

Chapter Two

The Unexpected

After we took multiple loads to the new apartment, we came upon a large television. So the three of us, two other men and I, positioned ourselves and lifted the TV. As soon as we lifted it, something happened. My right leg buckled.

"Hold on for a second. Could one of you switch positions with me? I need to catch my breath." I said.

"Sure. That's not a problem." one guy replied.

The two guys repositioned themselves so I could guide them up the stairs. I took as much pressure off my right leg as I possibly could. Maybe I should have eaten earlier. I thought to myself.

As we entered the apartment, I decided to rest for a moment. I felt somewhat fatigued so I leaned back on a chair. Time was of the essence so I stood up and attempted to take a step forward. Without warning I almost fell flat on my face. The others caught me with haste and sat me on the couch.

Everybody was confused about what just happened. We were desperate for a logical explanation. In the process, we discovered that my right leg went completely limp. Neither of us had any idea of what the issue might have been. As I sat on the couch I tried countless times to lift my leg, but it was hopeless. I struggled to hold myself up so they placed me on the carpet so I could lean my back against the couch.

Could it be a cramp or muscle spasm? I thought to myself. We figured it was minor so they continued to move the furniture. Moments later the others headed back to the old residence and left one of the guys behind with me. Before they left Ally squatted down and prayed with me. Ally then advised the young man to keep a close eye on me just in case matters grew worse.

As I sat on the carpet leaning sideways matters grew worse. What is going on? Why is this happening? What's wrong with me? What should I do? I thought to myself.

Moments later, I called a friend who worked at a hospital within the city.

"Hello." He answered.

"Hi Mike. I was helping someone move and my leg went totally limp. What do you think it might be?" I asked.

"It sounds like a muscle spasm. Grab a towel and wet it with hot water, hot as you can stand it. Roll it up and place it under your leg and let it sit for a while."

"Okay. Thanks. I'll see what I can find."

"Let me know what happen. I'll catch you later."

"Okay. I'll keep you posted."

"Bye-bye."

"Alright. Bye-bye."

So I hung up with him and sat puzzled all over again.

When it seemed things couldn't get any weirder, I had to use the bathroom. This can't be happening. I thought to myself. It was difficult to move so I asked the teen for help but he didn't know how to respond. As I positioned myself to lie on my belly; he froze for a moment and fear paralyzed him. So I literally crawled to the bathroom as I gripped the carpet with my left hand. It took forever it seemed.

After I made my way to the bathroom I attempted to stand. I struggled horribly so the teen stepped in. He held me up as I gained somewhat of a balance. I hopped to the toilet as I held onto the counter and shifted my weight to my left side.

I was exhausted! By the time I made it to the toilet, I had little to no strength left. My bladder was about to explode. I tried to balance myself as I reached for my belt with my left hand. As soon as I unbuckled my pants urine scattered everywhere. All I could do was shake my head. I was ashamed.

Never the less, I had the other guy assist me back to the living room. And then as I sat down, I looked up to heaven.

"God, whatever it is I'm facing, cover me. Please, don't let me die this way." I said.

Chapter Three

The Stroke Factor

As I leaned on the couch, for hours it seemed, the others returned from their second trip. They saw that matters grew worse so Ally called the paramedics. Within minutes they arrived and began to do a series of test. I was more nervous about the paramedics than anything else.

"Sir, what is your name?" the main paramedic asked, checking my vital signs as he looked at me.

"John." I replied.

"John, where are you right now?"

"I'm at a church member's new apartment."

"How old are you John?"

"I'm Twenty-five." Why so many questions? I thought to myself. Every so often he would ask the same question and I would give the same answer. I was somewhat annoyed by the repetition but I got over it rather quickly.

"John, are you experiencing any pain in your body?"

"No, I'm not."

"Do you have a headache, a migraine headache?"

"No sir, I don't have a headache."

"Is your body numb on either side?"

"No sir, not at all."

The two paramedics stood over me with a dumbfounded look on their faces. One of them applied pressure to my right leg.

"Can you feel that sir?" the paramedic asked.

"Yes sir, I can."

"Well John, we were trying to determine whether you had a stroke or not. Based on the test we ran, it can't be." he said. They began to pack up their equipment as they prepared to leave.

"Would you like to go to the hospital?" the paramedic asked. Before I had a chance to answer his question Ally made a phone call. She walked over to me and placed the cell phone to my ear.

The individual on the other end asked me several questions and I answered best that I could. Her response was direct.

"Go to the hospital." she said. By the serious tone of her voice, I just knew she wouldn't accept no for an answer.

It was the four words that changed my life.

So the paramedics began to strap me down.

"Would you like to go to Shand's or Baptist hospital?" he asked. I thought about it for a moment.

"Baptist hospital." I said. They continued to gather their things and rolled me down the stairs. We made it to the ambulance truck so they lifted me up and placed me inside. And off to Baptist Hospital we went. I was in the back of an ambulance truck accompanied by a paramedic and I had no idea why.

Within minutes we arrived at Baptist Hospital and the paramedics admitted me into the ER. Immediately the staff members grabbed hold of me and transported me to an empty room. And then they began to run various test. Minutes later, the doctor came into my room along with his staff. He had a clipboard in his hand and took a glance at it.

Everything appeared to be normal but things didn't add up. So the doctor requested that they do a CAT scan to find some sort of answer. They had me in that machine over an hour. I was so glad when it was over. Afterwards they took me back to my room.

Shortly after they ran the tests the doctor reentered my room. I was relaxed—uncomfortable but still calm about the situation.

"Mr. Mott, our CAT scan has revealed to us that you had a stroke." he said.

"Okay." I said. I sat calm as he attempted to give me his prognosis. My attitude really threw him and his staff members off. He continued to read aloud as he stood before me. There was a very disturbing look on his face.

"Mr. Mott, you had a brain hemorrhage which occurred on the left side of your body. We couldn't find a cause of why you had a stroke. I never encountered such a case before. You're very fortunate sir."

As I sat and listened, a smile came across my face.

"There's two major stroke types and you experienced the worse of the two, a hemorrhagic stroke which occurs due to a ruptured artery in the brain. What's amazing is that we usually perform open brain surgery due to the bleeding of the brain. Somehow your brain is healing itself." He began to smile as he looked at me. "You're very fortunate sir." he said.

I was speechless, at the same time thankful. I just knew that my God was in control. I took my mind back to when the incident first occurred; neither I— nor the doctors could find any possible reason of why I experienced a stroke. It was a miracle and my prayers have been answered. I thought to myself.

Chapter Four

Grace In My Space

What is grace? Why is it so important to me? I thought to myself. As I endured the obstacles associated with the stroke, the term *Grace* came to mind. There was one particular definition that stuck with me and I held it close to my heart. *Grace* is the love and favor that God shows towards people.

In my life I've had many issues arise and several disappointments. Even when things seemed unbearable, a form of support always made a difference. Sometimes it came in the form of people and in other instances in the form of situations.

I realized that life wasn't much if I had no one to share it with. Fortunately for me I had my church family by my side from the start. Minutes after the doctor left a married couple from my church stepped in the room. I was speechless. I was just admitted into the hospital and they managed to find me just that quick. Words could not express how much their presence meant to me.

We conversed briefly because the staff got word that multiple friends, family members and church members were in the lobby area to see me. Unfortunately, the staff had to send some of them home due to visitation policies. So the others left the hospital and came back at a later date.

I was so happy to see that the process would be much easier to bear because I had others grace me with their presence. I knew that everything would work itself out and that I would pull through the struggles that followed. The love and support alone made the process tolerable—not easy—but just a little easier to deal with.

After visitation hours the staff assigned me to a room. They plugged me into an IV and checked my vitals. Afterwards, the staff put me on three different medicines. Once they got me situated, they allowed friends and family to visit me. The phone rung off the hook and people stopped by frequently.

The most memorable moment was when my pastor, Bishop Goodman, stopped by and sat with me for a while. Of all the things he could have done, he spend time with me. He pictured me with tubes all over my body but it was the total opposite. I brought him up to speed far as my progress and I shared my experience with him. So we laughed and as always, he encouraged me. Before he left he touched the right side of my body from my shoulder to my foot as he spoke into my life.

My surroundings were occupied with space and that space was filled with loved ones. I felt that God graced with me with their presence when I needed it most. I wasn't crazy about the crowded room but I quickly adjusted. Words couldn't describe how I felt about the support I received.

The nurses stepped in periodically to check my vitals and supply my medication. I was poked so much that sleep became a thing of the past. Every three hours it seemed, they would step in and introduce themselves and then began the poke session. I had marks on both of my arms. What made it worse was that I never liked needles.

One particular day Mike stopped by my room. He was the same guy I got advice from prior to my hospital admission.

"Hey man. How's it going?" He asked.

"I'm doing alright. How about you?" I said. As I awaited his response, he began to sigh.

"I feel kind of bad. I wish there was something I could have done to help."

"Man, you did everything you could. It's not your fault. Just like I told everyone else, my God is in control!"

He took a deep breath.

"Yeah. Well, I just wanted to stop by and check up on you."

"Thanks man. I really appreciate it."

"No problem man. Let me get back to work. I'll catch you later."

"Okay. bro. Take care."

Every so often the staff would ask me about my expectations far as futuristic goals. It never failed, I looked them square in the eyes.

"I'm not settling for nothing less than one hundred percent." I said. I was paralyzed on one side of my body and yet I said that I wouldn't settle. I could only imagine what ran through their minds. After they heard it they did nothing more than smile and walk away. I was determined, nothing more, nothing less.

I've witnessed too many miracles in my life not to recognize one when I've seen it. At some point my mind took me back to when my deceased brother was alive. He battled with cancer at a very young age and as a result, he was paralyzed from the shoulders on down. The doctors told my mom that he would never walk again due to cancer and they asked her to relay the information to him. My mom refused to accept their prognosis and told him the very opposite.

And as a result, not long after that, my brother walked again. The doctors were blown away. They couldn't believe it. My mother's faith was strong and she reaped her reward which was to see him walk again for the last time. Even though my brother passed away, no one could deny that the grace of God was with him. As I reflected on my brother's short lived life, I realized that grace was in his space as it was in mine.

Chapter Five

Down But Not Out

There were times when I had no visitors or calls. I had what I call down time. The hospital had good movies which played throughout the day so I took advantage of it. I love martial arts, so when I saw that *Forbidden Kingdom* was played I couldn't resist.

I've always been an independent person. To rely on others meant dependency, I didn't like it one bit. If I wanted the bed adjusted I had to call in a nurse. If I was thirsty or had to use the bathroom the same thing applied. Over time I learned that my emotions carried little to no weight, so I adjusted and began to cooperate more.

I was not ungrateful, but I was uncomfortable. Even when it came to the hospital food I showed my gratitude by not complaining. I did possess some form of independence, when it came to eating I took full advantage of it. The food was half decent and I actually enjoyed it.

Even though I struggled to eat with my left hand, I had a peace about it. The dietary plan the staff had me on was bland. No more steaks and fries. I thought to myself. It wasn't as bad as I thought it was. I was just use to having what I wanted when I wanted it.

There was one particular term that rarely surfaced in the hospital and I quickly discovered what it was. The term sleep was more of a foreign language. Every time I closed my eyes I was awakened from my sleep. The nurses checked my vitals around the clock. I never had to work so hard to get sleep before. I had to get it when I could and it was a challenge.

I made continuous progress throughout the process and I was so grateful. It could have been worse than what it was. There were moments that made my stay more pleasant. One of which was that I had the privilege of meeting a Jaguar cheerleader. I didn't know it until she left my room, but that's beside the point.

I thought it was awesome that cheerleaders did such a thing. I tried to take a picture with her but it didn't happen. She was far gone once I found out about her. That would have been great! I would have added the picture to my collection of memorable moments.

The staff at Baptist was great. They catered to my every need. My discharge was at hand so they gathered my things to prepare me. I was there six days and they already had a therapy rehab in mind. I had all the more reason to smile and be thankful.

The calendar read April 2nd and the paramedics arrived armed and ready. They quickly transported me to the ambulance truck and hauled me to Brooks Rehabilitation Hospital. The time of which I spent at Baptist was on a whole different scale compared to my experience at Brooks Rehab. When we arrived the paramedics transported me to the third floor which was the stroke floor.

After I got settled in on came the paperwork. My case manager stepped in and briefed me on my stay at Brooks. She explained my options concerning my insurance benefits. Everything seemed okay until my health provider encountered issues with my stay at Brooks. When all was said and done, my health provider agreed to cover my expenses for sixteen days.

I soon found out that my position was terminated due to my leave of absence. My manager immediately stepped in and took action. And as any Christian would do, I prayed and left it in God's hands. Needless to say, when the cookie crumbled...I still had my job.

I had multiple things occur all at the same time. After we got past the paperwork the staff then introduced themselves. Not long after that the nurse came in to check my vitals. Moments later a speech therapist entered my room. She had no idea what she was in for. Why is she here? I thought to myself. After she introduced herself and walked through a warm-up exercise. She looked at me in amazement.

"Mr. Mott, you don't need speech therapy." she said. I couldn't do nothing but laugh. She left and made her way down the hallway. Within minutes my case manager appeared and showed me around the rehab hospital. She gave me a list of my doctors, therapist, and nurses. Afterwards I was given my three medications.

Later that afternoon the dietician brought in a menu so that I could place my order. At first I was hesitant but when I sunk my teeth down into the food I was convinced otherwise. I was on a strict diet due to my stroke and I didn't like that one bit. I must admit, their food was the best hospital food I ever had.

The next day I devoted time to make calls to let the others know about the transition from Baptist to Brooks Rehab. I was thankful that I had others aid me throughout the process. Without hesitation they stepped in and assisted me in multiple ways. My church family played a major role in my life as I went through the process. I had everything I needed for my stay at Brooks Rehab. Even though I appeared to have been down at times, I was never out.

Chapter Six

The Power Of Influence

Weekends were slow because therapy sessions were held on weekdays only. The same applied to doctor visits as well. Saturday's were geared towards group therapy activities. Group activities were put together to get others to interact with one another. As we got acquainted we were then able to open up more for various discussions.

Each of us shared personal stories and how our stroke experience impacted our lives. As I examined the room, there was one thing that was apparent to me at that moment, there were several angry and depressed people. Some of them allowed their frustration to make them bitter. And others refused to cooperate.

When I saw it I immediately processed it in my mind. And I then attempted to resolve the issue by changing the atmosphere. My main objective was to get their minds off their situation. As funny as it sounds, my aim was to expose them to laughter. If I could get them to laugh then I would have them just where I wanted them. I thought to myself.

At times I would crack random jokes to break the ice. I smiled a lot, especially when I was around negative people. Sometimes all it took was a simple smile along with a warm greeting. I always asked for the person's name to show them that I was sincere about it. It really made a difference. I thought that it was important to address a person by name so I put forth the effort to do so.

I found it somewhat difficult at first to reach out to them because the stroke affected us differently. Some patients couldn't talk while others had a speech impediment. Some had memory problems and others were outright negative. There were a few who truly appreciated what I did and they showed their gratitude.

I had a tough audience but I did not allow that to intimidate me. I kept a smile on my face and made the most of it. To do what I did, I had to have had the right frame of mind. I took time to really examine my surroundings. Only then was I able to look at the big picture. As a result, I took the attention off me and placed it on others—the big picture.

Sundays were hard for me. I was use to church service not a hospital. Typically I would get up first thing in the morning, freshen up and make my way to The Temple at One Accord Ministries Int'l. I was uneasy about it. I looked forward to the word of God. It changed my life.

I felt as though I committed a sin of some sort—okay, maybe I went overboard, it just didn't seem right. My life has never been the same since I became a member at One Accord Ministries. Those who know me would be the first to admit it. If I wasn't under the influence of Bishop Dr. Jan D. Goodman Sr., my experience and the outcome would have been totally different—period!

When I came to grips with reality, far as church attendance, I took the alternative route. Since I couldn't attend church service, I asked others to call me so I could hear it by phone. I was determined! The familiar voices were like medicine to my soul. It was a pleasant experience and I was thankful for it.

If I did have unpleasant moments, after my bishop's message, they didn't exist anymore. The lively music moved me and the beautiful voices comforted me as they song in harmony. The icing on the cake, so to speak, was the booming voice of my pastor who closed out the service with a phenomenal message which pierced my soul.

I could hardly wait for my discharge. The thought of church excited me. I pictured myself in church continuously. I knew that shortly after I heard the service by phone that church members would come visit me. As always, the calls began and the random visits. It was so much love expressed in multiple ways.

The excitement radiated throughout my room as they entered from the hallway. Without fail, they shared their experiences from church service. I couldn't help but smile as they graced me with their presence. It made me happy to have had people visit me and express their love in more ways than one.

I got all that I could when others visited me. No matter how great the moment was, when they left my presence, I was by myself all over again. So I interacted with them, showed my interest and I was excited. As they wrapped up their visit the laughs came to a halt. And the farewells followed as they left my room.

And then there would be complete silence. Usually I prayed or meditated on God's word to make the most of it. Eventually I tossed and turned until sleep fell upon me. Often times it took hours to go to sleep. When I did, I took full advantage of it.

As soon as I shut my eyes, it never failed, either a nurse or their assistant would enter my room and disturb my sleep. They checked my vitals and changed my I-V. I never liked needles, so when they poked me, I would look away and sigh at times. The frequent nurse visits were the most frustrating part of my stay at Brooks Rehab. After a while I got used to it.

On one particular Monday, I awakened from my sleep as the therapist addressed me.

"Good morning Mr. Mott. It's eight o'clock. Are you ready for therapy?" the therapist said.

"Good morning. Yes I am" I said. They insisted that I got dressed quickly. They did give me some independence and allowed me to dress myself. I struggled a little at first.

"Do you need any help? the therapist asked.

"No thank you. I got it." I replied. I knew that it was important for me to have had some independence. So I intentionally did some things by myself. It took me a while but I developed a measure of self-reliance.

For sixteen days it was the same routine. At eight o'clock each morning, weekday mornings, I made my way to the gym for occupational therapy. Physical therapy followed right after my first session. The therapist always introduced themselves by name prior to the sessions. The atmosphere was positive and filled with professional staff members.

The sessions were intense but I was determined. The kindness of the therapist made things more tolerable. And because of that, I was able to bond with the therapist and at the same time impact the lives of other stroke patients. I made it my business to be a light to others by bringing them hope and I have God to thank for that. I discovered that influence is everything—mainly positive influence.

Chapter Seven

Determined

As time progressed, I grew attached to certain therapist throughout the process. It wasn't that the other therapist slacked; it was that some had a closer bond than others. Maybe it was their personality. Or maybe it was their sense of humor. I always loved a good laugh. It could have been their work ethic or passion for what they did.

All I knew was that my life has been greatly impacted by them. It took a special group of people to have captured my heart and undivided attention and that's just what they did. Someway, somehow they made me feel as though I could have conquered the world. My therapists were incredible and they helped me every step of the way.

There were days when I wanted to sit down and do nothing or just quit. My therapist always found ways to tap into my inner strength and encouraged me. I quickly found out that *I can't* was forbidden. At Brooks Rehab, they wouldn't accept defeat, so quitting wasn't an option. One of my first objectives was to change my vocabulary.

I was well educated on the terms and what they meant. My physical therapist was originally Rhonda but Michael eventually stepped in. Physical therapy dealt with normal functions of the body such as agility and movement. My occupational therapist was Amy Stover at the time. It dealt more with daily living activities such as cleaning, bathing, and job related functions.

I felt like a baby all over again. I went through the stages of physical development once again. Far as my recovery went, I made rapid improvement and the staff was fascinated. I bumped my head quite a few times—figuratively speaking—I had my sights on full recovery. I looked at the scars as reminders and the temporary failures as motivators.

One particular morning I made my way to the gym and met with Becky my physical therapist.

"Okay Mr. Mott. I'll do the exercise first and then I want you to do the same." Becky said.

"Okay." I replied. We began the exercises and I got exhausted rather quickly. I was short on breath and I wanted to quit.

"Come on Mr. Mott, give me a few more."

"I can't"

"I know you can do it. If you're just tired, you have a few more left in you. Now if you're not feeling well just let me know." Becky said. Afterwards I stuck it out and continued the exercises. I was worn out when it was over with, so I made my way to my room to recuperate.

Every so often church members would sit in on my therapy sessions. Whenever I saw their faces it motivated me even the more. They were blown away by my recovery. I jumped leaps and bounds far as my recovery rate. My therapist were amazed at how much progress I made in such a short period of time.

I actually enjoy being here. I thought to myself one day. It's not that I would have wanted to relive my experience because I wouldn't. I was so impressed with the structure and atmosphere of Brooks Rehab and I wanted to be a part of it somehow.

I loved to play sports so I was in high hopes of full recovery. I was very energetic prior to the stroke and my experience put that on hold for quite some time. I felt as though I was stripped of my natural abilities. I knew that my recovery would take time and that the process would be difficult. I would take deep breaths and role with the punches because quitting wasn't an option.

Chapter Eight

Laser Focused

I was never the type of person to overlook others in order to benefit myself. Through my eyes, I looked at things differently. I felt as though helping others was actually helping myself. My whole objective was to aid others through my process no matter what.

I made it my duty to be selfless in order to cut out selfish activities. I realized that everybody needs somebody and I happen to be that somebody others needed in their moments of despair. I was fortunate enough to have loved ones support me through my situation, some patients had no support at all. I was eager to encourage, others even when it seemed helpless I made an attempt.

I recall when I when I was given permission to wheel myself throughout the hospital. I took full advantage of it. I have always been the talkative type and throughout my experience I made no exceptions. When the opportunity arose I didn't hesitate, I made my way to the hallway and encouraged folks.

Whenever I detected discomfort or distress from others I would console that person. I remember when I got on the elevator and made my way to another floor. When I got off the elevator I encountered a young lady and after I conversed with her, I immediately consoled her. I wrapped up the conversation and began to make my way to the elevator.

"Goodnight. See you tomorrow." the young lady said.

"Okay. Goodnight." I replied. I had no idea if I would ever see her again. I moved on and made my way back to my room and went to sleep. What it all boiled down to was that I did what any kind hearted person would do and that was to make a difference. And I believed that every person I came in contact with was impacted by our encounter to some extent.

One afternoon I made my way to the waterfall outside of the hospital. It was a sight to see. It had beautiful gold fish which swam around, aged statues and a waterfall. I sat for hours it seemed. The calmness of the water was soothing and it took my mind off my situation. I had inner peace and that's all that mattered at that moment.

There were times when I thought of the misfortunes of others. It made me more grateful to be in the state that I was in. My recovery rate was unheard of. I couldn't help but empathize with other stroke patients because their condition was more likely severe compared to mine. I had God to thank for that.

There were different groups at Brooks Rehab such as the stroke group. They came to us to monitor our progress and make the activities somewhat fun. Every so often the stroke group chose selected individuals to join them on field trips. To my surprise, I was chosen to go along with them one day. So they rolled us down to the first floor and loaded us unto the vehicle.

Afterwards we made our way to a supermarket and were given instructions. Our task was to pick up items which were on the list and then return them. When we were finished they questioned us about our experience and we gave our feedback. The whole thing was geared towards independence, nothing more and nothing less.

Another study I participated in was weird. It was a laugh session that the group participated in. It took me a moment to adjust but I made the most of it. And then it hit me, it was pure genius! What better way to lift the patient's spirits than to take their mind off their situations. I thought to myself.

Laugher is like medicine to the soul and at Brooks Rehab, it was a rare commodity—far as stroke patients. Each of us had to develop our own unique laugh that others had to mimic. Afterwards we had the next person do the same. The objective was to claim the winner with the most unique laugh. The winner was then announced and we went our separate ways.

One day as I laid in bed my cellphone began to ring. I was excited at first and I gave my undivided attention to the person on the other end. To my surprise, it was heartbreaking news; a dear friend, more like an uncle, passed away. The person on the other end discussed all the details about the home going service. The service was the following Saturday and I just had to be there. So I spoke with the staff and they looked into it.

Fortunately they were able to pull a few strings for me. It was a very tough time for me emotionally so every bit of comfort helped significantly. I dealt with my own situation and lost a close friend all at the same time. Arrangements were made which consisted of my friend who was to pick me up so we could attend the home going service.

I was able to encourage the family at the home going service despite my emotional state of mind. It was nice to have seen so many familiar faces. And the service went exceptionally well.

After engaging the family members I made my way back to the car along with my friend. We had a four hour window so we hurried back to the rehab hospital.

I felt better because I was able to give my condolences to the family. I reflected on the good memories I had with him and tried not to let it get me down. I didn't have the privilege of getting to know him personally but I had my brief moments with him and they were impactful. Without a doubt in my mind he left behind a great legacy. Moments after reminiscing, I realized how exhausted I was and I decided to go to sleep.

Sunday came and I could hardly wait for my cell phone to ring because I just knew what was next. That's right, the word of God! I got excited because every time I heard the word preached by Bishop Goodman it did something to me, it made me better and it made me stronger. No matter how my day went prior to it, my spirit was lifted. I felt as though I was in Sunday service and I enjoyed every moment of it.

As time elapsed I continued to recover rapidly which enabled me to do more exercises. I transitioned from dependency to independence in a matter of days. My arm seemed to have made greater progress than my leg so we focused more on my leg exercises. Due to the limitations on my right side, I had to adjust and use my left side. It was very difficult but I began to improve over time.

As a writer, I found it to be almost impossible to keep my thoughts on paper. I got frustrated at times because my handwriting was horrible. My thoughts came far quicker than the pace of which I wrote. So to keep myself calm I decided to hold off from writing. The last thing I needed was to allow negativity to invade my space.

I had other moments at Brooks Rehab which were not so pleasant but I kept the end result in mind. When I took showers, it was pretty interesting far as normality. It didn't take long for me to realize that I had no privacy because I had none. I was so embarrassed when the nurses bathed me but I had to be clean. Far as I was concerned, I had no other choice. So I swallowed pride and cooperated.

I had to keep in mind that the staff was only doing their job, nothing more and nothing less; when I looked at it from that perspective things went a lot smoother. Eventually I found humor in my situation and I laughed about it. I turned to humor when I had nothing else to look forward to. All I did was turn lemons into lemonade. I discovered that time waited on no one so I aimed to use it wisely and made the most out of it. I did this by impact which came when I encouraged others.

I also observed my surroundings and I saw that others had conditions far worse than mine. For those who had less severe conditions, the outcome was about the same, most of them were negative. For myself, my cure was laughter and others couldn't help but acknowledge it. If I didn't smile than something was wrong—seriously wrong.

There were three words that stuck with me as I endured my stroke experience, "mind over matter", these words impacted my life in a major way. The phrase rung volumes in my ear and I could not dismiss it. I made up my mind to recover from the start, not when progress was made. I released my faith and trusted God. I told myself that it was only a season and that the best was bound to come.

No matter what I faced, I always set a positive atmosphere. The stroke was a lot to deal with and the last thing I needed was for more stress to be added. Before I transitioned from the bed to the wheelchair, I saw myself walking. Even when some doubted and others worried, I pressed my way through the negativity. I had a choice to have accepted defeat or to have stood on my beliefs—I chose to stand on my beliefs. And that came by consistent focus, action and prayer.

Chapter Nine

Progress In The Making

I was used to eating regular foods before my stroke experience. After the stroke, that changed instantly. I had to adjust and alter my eating habits. It was a challenge a sure. My dietician put together a plan which consisted of lightly seasoned foods and plenty of veggies. I was deeply disturbed by it.

Fortunately for me, because of my rapid recovery, I was able to eat on a broader scale. One afternoon a gentleman with a snack cart stopped by my room.

"Would you like any snacks sir?" he asked.

I could barely contain myself. I looked at him as I smiled.

"Yes I would. What type of snacks do you have?" I asked.

"I have peanut butter crackers, chips, yogurt, ice cream, cookies and different types of juice."

I grabbed a little bit of everything.

"Thanks sir. I appreciate it."

"No problem." he said." He then grabbed the push cart and exited my room. Days later the same thing occurred but I had a visitor present with me. We nearly cleaned him out. I was somewhat ashamed but he had no problem with it so we continued to grab more items.

One particular afternoon I was accompanied by a few church members. We laughed and joked as we reflected on my continuous growth up to that very moment. At random I received a call from a fellow church member. On the way to visit me she stopped by Popeye's Chicken.

"Hi Deacon Mott! I'm at Popeye's. Would you like me to get you anything?" she asked. At first I hesitated.

"I would love some but let me check with the hospital first." I said.

"Okay. That would be the best thing to do." she said. Minutes later I was given permission to do so; I was able to sink my teeth down into some Popeye's Chicken. I immediately called her back to relay the message. So she ordered me a red bean and rice chicken bowl.

I developed a daily routine which worked out pretty well. I would wake up and make my way to the bathroom. I then freshened up and put on my workout clothes. Every look in the mirror reminded me of how bad I needed a haircut. I laughed at myself often because the chia pet commercial was the first thing which came to mind. All I had to do was add water and watch it grow. Thankfully there was a barber at my church who volunteered her services.

The more I improved, the more aggressive the sessions became. I used humor to get through the long and exhausting exercises. As time progressed I developed a bond with certain therapists. Our relationship was very unique. We cracked jokes on each other every chance we got—mainly me. I couldn't slack because I knew that if I did they would crack jokes on me. Others would look on and often times they got a piece of the action.

There was never a dull moment when it came to therapy. From start to finish I found humor in almost everything. When I approached the gym, it never failed, someone would break the ice and we all laughed aloud. It got to the point wherein the therapist begged me to stop because they could no longer contain themselves. I knew that humor took the focus off the individual's problems so I used it as an outlet.

I also read the Bible to keep myself in the right frame of mind. As I read the scriptures it took my mind far beyond my circumstances. I feed my stomach but it was just as important for me to have feed my spirit man. There was so many negative patients around and I had to regroup somehow. At the end of the day, the Bible served its purpose and impacted my life.

My stay at Brooks Rehab was brief and discharge came rather quickly. I spent sixteen days there and every second counted. My case manager worked with my insurance company to prepare for my discharge date. My last day was scheduled for April 18th and I could hardly wait.

I was supposed to leave at 11 a.m. so I packed my belongings and proceeded to the first floor. Before I left the rehab, they made a customized AFO brace for my right leg. Along with that, they gave me a shower chair and walker cane. I also contacted my employer and brought them up to speed.

Prior to my discharge, I communicated with my leasing office at the apartment complex of my residence. Since I lived on the second floor I thought to see what options I had available. So I briefed them on my situation and then I waited patiently. To my surprise, they found another apartment downstairs and waived my transfer fee. I couldn't help but smile and flow with the process.

Afterwards, I relayed the information to my church members, family and friends. A handful of my church members were nice enough to move my furniture from the old apartment to the new apartment. With the help of Brooks Rehab, family and friends, my transition from rehab to home went smoothly.

When I was discharged a friend dropped me off to my apartment. After we arrived we took in my items from the rehab. Shortly after I had three core people meet with me and they aided me through the entire process. They put together a schedule to keep track of my outpatient therapy sessions and paper.

I was assigned sixteen visits to the outpatient rehab center. Several calls were made so that others could assist in process. I didn't have to worry about anything; from laundry to food, I was covered. I wasn't accustomed to others taking care of me so I had to adjust to it.

The doctors wrote my prescriptions and they also set up follow up appointments. One of the first things we did was get the prescriptions. There were three different type of medicines. After we picked up the medicines, we made arrangements to attend therapy and doctor appointments.

Days later, I took a trip to the grocery store. It felt good to pick out what I wanted to eat for a change. I was so accustom to hospital food and I could hardly wait to consume a home cooked meal. I did eat salty foods occasionally but I took my medication as advised and went to therapy regularly.

There wasn't a time wherein I didn't think of church. Monday thru Friday I attended therapy sessions and I rested on Saturday. Well, not rest necessarily, but I did slow things down. When Sunday came I was like a kid in a candy store. I just knew that I would be blessed by the message from my pastor.

As usual, I was awakened by the sound of my alarm clock. It was Sunday morning, my first Sunday since I arrived home from the rehab hospital. I made up my bed and said a prayer. I then sorted out my clothing and freshened up for church in swift motion. After greeting each other, one of my caregivers and I ate breakfast before we left my apartment.

We pulled off and headed to church; we were headed to The Temple at One Accord Ministries International Inc. I was so anxious to see everybody and I longed to be in the midst of other believers. As we exited the car, I slowly stood to my feet. When we got to the stairs, I sighed as I took my first step. Minutes later I entered The Temple and immediately I felt the love of my church family.

My church had many nicknames; the loving church was just one of them. With that being said, I was probably hugged close to forty times before I even made it to my seat. Church service began and the atmosphere was set so I joined in as I often did. I got my praise on despite my limitations on my right side. And as expected, my pastor delivered a life changing message to all who was present.

As time moved on, so did my progress. My first week of outpatient therapy arrived and I was ready to take on any challenge that was set before me. From day one, I noticed that outpatient therapy was far more intense than inpatient therapy. As I exercised, my right arm began to improve more rapidly than my leg. At first I was disturbed by it but I eventually got over it.

One particular Sunday something happened. After service I approached my pastor as I often did. I thanked him and embraced him as well. Without warning he placed his hands on my shoulders. He looked me square in the eyes and challenged me to no longer rely on the cane I had.

At that moment, I made my decision. The following week I approached him as I did before, without the cane. Others looked on and questioned me about not having the cane. I did not allow that to place doubt in my mind because I knew that I made the right decision. My pastor saw me exercise my faith yet again and he was Godly proud of me.

Around the same period of time I spoke with my AFLAC agent to see if I could benefit from my policy I had with them. To my surprise, I had accidental coverage rather than disability insurance. It was heart reckoning. I got over it rather quickly and things began to work themselves out. Everything I needed came one way or another and for that I was grateful.

I continued to attend my doctor appointments in between my therapy sessions and church. Far as appointments, the doctors were impressed with the progress I made. I had nothing but good reports from each of my doctor visits. My health was intact; it was as if I never had a stroke.

Chapter Ten

A Fight To The Finish

Although I believed in divine healing, I had enough common sense to know that God gave doctors the ability to help in the healing process. I knew that the medicine given to me would aid me along the way. I took my medicine as prescribed by my doctor and I did it consistently. After my first refill, I no longer needed the medicine. The doctors saw rapid improvement in my health and weaned me from all three medications

I did not allow the rapid improvements get to my head, instead I saw it as a motivational tool. I continued my therapy sessions no matter how tough things became. There were times wherein progress seemed to have come to a standstill. After my sixteen sessions were over, I exercised at the fitness center within my apartment complex. Never the less, I kept the same determined mindset that I had from the very beginning.

When I finished with outpatient therapy things began to slow down. I was too bored, so I spoke with my doctors to be cleared to go back to work. Shortly after, my desire was granted so I ran it by my employer. Is this a wise decision? I thought to myself. My mind was set and it was no turning back.

When I went back to work things were different. The strenuous activity took a lot out of me. I was required to lift, stoop and squat along with other duties. At first, things seemed okay because I got what I wanted which was to go back to work. At the warehouse where I worked, others relied on me a lot so I had to move at a steady pace. I began to doubt the decision I made of going back to work.

We lifted heavy machinery all the time and it was a quick paced environment. Everything seemed tolerable until one day as I lifted a copier, a sharp pain ran through my right foot. Every time I lifted something heavy my toes would cringe and severe pain followed. Matters grew worse so two and a half months later I resigned—on my birthday.

I got with a doctor at a clinic and they informed me that I had an ingrown toenail on my big toe. The friction, moisture and muscle compensation was the cause of it. In other words, whenever I lifted something my stronger muscles would compensate for the weaker ones. And friction came about when my toes cringed.

After he gave me insight on my condition, he decided to do outpatient surgery the same day of my visit. His assistant prepped while he looked over the paperwork. They started the process by numbing my toe. Minutes later they were done and they began to wrap my toe with bandages. And just in case the pain surfaced, they gave me pain pills.

They then billed me for the procedure. I was thankful that I set up a 401k account before I left the company I recently worked for. I didn't have much funds but every penny helped. After I left my job I no longer had health insurance. To cover some of my expenses, I applied for disability and without fail I was denied.

If I learned nothing else, I discovered that God was with me throughout my life changing experience. When I attempted to do things my way they crumbled up and failed. Every door I tried to open slammed in my face. When I applied for health insurance I could not obtain it. And when I got some money I spent it foolishly.

With no income, I found myself homeless and helpless. No matter how bad it seemed, I knew I could make one phone call and some of my worries would fade away. The only thing was that I was accustom to living alone but I swallowed my pride and made the call.

I moved back to my parent's house and made the most out of it. It felt as though I made one step forward only to make two steps backward.

All I could do was pray and stay the course. Even though I felt as if God didn't hear me at times, I knew that I would overcome the odds. I admit, I had my moments and I made several mistakes along the way. I realized something throughout my recovery; I learned that in my defining moment I found out what I was truly made of.

While others acknowledged the strength and determination of my character, I had to live with the regret of taking my caregivers for granted. It was the small things that counted most and at first, I didn't realize it. I thought I had all the answers but I was wrong. I saw the tears roll off the cheeks of one individual and the stress level of another intensify. I owed those individuals an apology so I approached each one of them.

I made bad decisions at times and those decisions affected everyone connected to me. When I swallowed pride, only then was I able to make the necessary changes. After I admitted my wrong and humbled myself, my loved ones expressed their love more freely. And freely I received it.

I looked beyond the dark clouds and saw the light. Things started to line up for me—and for me, it was timely. I applied for government assistance and I received a free phone. I also qualified for food stamps and I had plenty. I didn't get all I desired but I was grateful.

One afternoon I stumbled across an opportunity to earn money so I took the initiative. I became a salesman in hope of decent income. I made little to no money but some was better than none. At least it keeps me busy. I thought to myself.

When my customer base dwindled down, I pursued other things. I volunteered at Brooks Rehab every Friday. One afternoon I was approached by a staff member. They mentioned that there was another rehab center nearby and I could utilize their facility for free. I wanted to strengthen my right side more so I took advantage of it. I regained focus and exercised on a weekly basis.

Not long after that, a friend and I enrolled in culinary arts at a technical college. Weeks later, the both of us were accepted at two different country clubs as interns. I transitioned from an intern to a full-time employee within months. I went to the rehab center on my off days, which were three times a week. I enjoyed the moment while it lasted and I sharpened my cooking skills.

The school was incredible but I knew that I was living someone else's dream. So I quit going to the school and weeks later I was laid off my job at the country club.

I lost my job due to circumstances beyond my control. Things became sour all over again. Despite my issues, I made it to rehab and I volunteered consistently.

Every time I made progress, I found some sort of distraction. I didn't see the improvements because I interrupted the process. I ignored the problem because I was too busy to have noticed it. When I removed the distractions, only then was I able to see clearly. And then it hit me; I needed to allow the healing process to take its course.

On the other hand, I enrolled in the Neuro-recovery program at Brooks Rehab. I was determined to complete it. Every week progress was made. My faith and determination allowed me to stand among others who had the same mind-set. I knew it wouldn't be easy so I pressed my way.

Furthermore, I had three goals in mind; to show my gratitude towards the staff, to impact the lives of other stroke victims and to fully recover from the stroke. I knew it would be one day at a time. Even though I was down, I wasn't out for the count. With God's grace in my life, I was bound to pull through. I would not settle for anything less than one hundred percent. I knew with determination and willpower I could do it!